THE BREAKAGE

Glyn Maxwell

ff

faber and faber

First published in 1998
by Faber and Faber Limited
3 Queen Square London WC1N 3AU

Photoset by Wilmaset Ltd, Birkenhead, Wirral
Printed in England by Mackays of Chatham plc, Chatham, Kent

A CIP record for this book
is available from the British Library

ISBN 0-571-19337-4

10 9 8 7 6 5 4 3 2 1

Glyn Maxwell

for Geraldine

CONTENTS

THE BREAKAGE

THE BREAKAGE

Someone broke our beautiful
      All-coloured window. They were saints
He broke, or she or it broke. They were
      Colours you can't get now.

Nothing else was touched. Only our
      Treasured decoration, while it
Blackened in its calm last night, light
      Dead in it, like He is.

Now needles of all length and angle
      Jab at air. They frame a scene
Of frosty meadows, all our townsmen
      Bobbing here to mourn this,

To moan and wonder what would mount
      And ride so far to grieve us,
Yet do no more than wink and trash,
      Not climb down in here even.

Most eyes are on the woods, though,
      Minds on some known figures.
At least until they too turn up here,
      Sleep-white, without stories.

Things it could have done in here
      It hasn't done. It left it all
The way it was, in darkness first, now
      This, the dull light day has.

We kneel and start. And blood comes
      Like luck to the blue fingers
Of children thinking they can help,
      Quick as I can warn them.

[3]

AN AUGUST MONDAY

It's going to take forever for the holiday
That got all spoiled to ever happen properly.

The day was bright and blue and when a day like that
Goes wrong it's not your fault it's other people's fault.

Mother says there's other days we'll do the same
As what we wanted. I don't think that *is* the same

As doing it before. Sunday and Saturday
Were both a wash-out and a waste of holiday

Which meant we had one chance to go and this was it.
Packed our picnic hamper, couldn't hardly fit

The stuff we wanted in! We had a hansom cab
I helped to load. I don't mind doing any job

I can if I can see it gets us on our way.
And nothing beats the seaside on a sunny day.

I said that in the cab around Trafalgar Square,
Where everyone was on the way to everywhere,

But if you're blinking asking then I'm telling you
How far we got. Approximately Waterloo.

I'd seen it once or twice but now you couldn't move
For people in your way *Now mind yourself there love*

And sailors shaking hands, one man in army rig
Too small for him, we had to laugh, he looked so big,

And him who'd chalked a message on a dirty board
That said NO SPECIAL TRAINS, I do hereby award

The first of my three prizes. They're for services
To ruining my day and what the sentence is

Is that he's going to get these special fingernails
That everything they touch is changed until it feels

Like what a blackboard's made of. Now he'll always hear
Screeching, won't he. Father had the next idea,

To see the wax exhibits of the kings and all
Of Austria they'd put in some old stuffy hall

The other side of London. When we saw the queue
Go clean around the block we said we did tell you

And all those people standing there get second prize,
Which is to turn to wax of course, except their eyes

And they stay real, and when the sun begins to beat
On them the way it did on us on Baker Street

The eyes are all they'll be. They'll wish they hadn't said
Let's see the kings of Austria the day we did.

Victoria, now father told the taxi bloke,
I said she's made of wax though no one got the joke!

The station, he said, sweating, I remember now.
He'd get one of my prizes if it weren't for how

He did keep trying to think of things to save the day,
But always like museums and that. We had to say

That wasn't going to happen. We thought Waterloo
Was bad. Victoria was like a blinking zoo

With barriers and every kind of monkey sort
All round the ticket hall. My older sister thought

[5]

They could be captured burglars being shown to trains
To take them to their prisons but they'd got no chains

I pointed out and mother said *Don't point*, then said
They'd all got people somewhere. *How about dead ahead*

Said uncle and we saw them in a shabby line,
The families, by a hoarding with an arrow sign.

And when their men came back I shouted *Butchers, bakers!*
While mother shook her head to stop me *Candlemakers!*

Them being still all dressed in what they did all day.
Which made it so amazing they were going away.

And father had no tickets when he hurried back,
And said there's no excursions on and every track

Was taken for the Channel trains. And that was that.
No prizes now for guessing who is going to get

My top award for ruining that holiday.
And what they get is that they've got to go away

Always, that there's not a place the train can stop.
No town, no ticket-man, no empty butcher shop

To start again in! Worst of all, they'll never see
Me again which means they'll have to cease to be,

The way I see it. Now they'll wish they'd turn to wax,
Or scratch their way wherever with that dreaded scratch

The other got from me. By now we'd had enough.
We settled for Hyde Park and spread our picnic stuff

The way we would have had a single thing that day
Gone right, the way we would have done on Durlston Bay,

Played cricket and made apple cup like every year.
Had everyone not made a pact to keep us here.

Late sun we had, stale sandwiches and hardly space
To sit in and a young man with a country face

Right next to us kept dozing on our bit of rug
And kicking and he broke my Coronation mug

Which ought to get him something of a special prize
But I was tired of doing that and shut my eyes,

And dreamed about our day the way it should have gone.
No one was standing in the way of anyone.

We saw the sea from well inland, a vale of blue
There suddenly between two hills, it grew and grew

Until the land gave in and all we saw was gold
Before us and a silver rail of light unrolled

Our way from the horizon as we reached the sea
And dug for shells and listened to them patiently,

Then threw them back and raced to where the hamper now
Stood up and opened, no one seemed to wonder how,

But started tucking in until the signal went
To hurry to what uncle called the main event.

Big men in blazers guided us along the prom
Towards a lawn with everyone from where we're from

And no exceptions, even those we couldn't find
We knew were somewhere, nobody'd been left behind,

And even those we'd seen and their pathetic things
That day had instruments with gold embellishings,

[7]

Which when the whistle blew they stood and played for us
A waltz we know, which then does what it always does:

Turns to one high trumpet, then a drum and then
Shellfire, which is what it is, round Valenciennes.

AS A GHOST WOULD MAKE YOU

His aged desk, or his Cheshire map by now
gone Middle Eastern ochre; polish sprayed
and slapped in the gleam of some prim, livid decade;
guns on a wall, a Wisden. We all know

these things might do it, unconceal a smell:
in the giddying of a boy be culpable,
as you sniff it grown one day. You would need your brother,
whatever it means to him, to tag that aroma

somehow. What can erase it but to breathe it
briskly and fully now as a ghost would make you?
Face the thing with a casual 'I believe this,'
nodding it in till it goes away or you have to.

All around, an oven of smell is making
memory of the moment, and you can't
be part of that. You smile and have learned nothing,
like you in a photo. Already a babbling infant

is getting it without you, all her features
set by smell. One day she'll have that look
again and sniff and something will approach her,
quicken her breath, unearth you for a second.

MY GRANDFATHER AT THE POOL

i.m. James Maxwell 1895–1980

This photo I know best of him is him
With pals of his about to take a swim,

Forming a line with four of them, so five
All told one afternoon, about to dive:

Merseysiders, grinning and wire-thin,
Still balanced, not too late to not go in,

Or feint to but then teeter on a whim.
The only one who turned away is him,

About to live the trenches and survive,
Alone, as luck would have it, of the five.

Four gazing at us levelly, one not.
Another pal decided on this shot,

Looked down into the box and said *I say*
And only James looked up and then away.

I narrow my own eyes until they blur.
In a blue sneeze of a cornfield near Flers

In 1969, he went *Near here*

It happened and he didn't say it twice.
It's summer and the pool will be like ice.

Five pals in Liverpool about to swim.
The only one who looks away is him.

The other four look steadily across
The water and the joke they share to us.

[10]

Wholly and coldly gone, they meet our eyes
Like stars the eye is told are there and tries

To see — all pity flashes back from there,
Till I too am the unnamed unaware

And things are stacked ahead of me so vast
I sun myself in shadows that they cast:

Things I dreamed but never dreamed were there,
But are and may by now be everywhere,

When you're what turns the page or looks away.
When I'm what disappears into my day.

ENGLAND GERMANY

The boys were risen right out of their seats
By the wind the whistle cued, they pushed along
In the damp and heavy-coated crowd away
From all of it, away from this one song
The man beside them knew. Rough cigarettes
He'd prodded at them while he had his say
About the action. Now where was he gone,
They wondered. Not so far: he'd only paused
A sec to cup a hand to his white face
As the flame he got kept blowing out. This caused
The men behind to eff and blind this one
Obstruction tottering in the one place
They had to be. In good part the boys too
Had something left to share with him: some crack
About his not-in-fact-that-lucky stone.
But when they turned again he still hung back,
Striking and striking as men muscled through
Obscuring him, till he became unknown.

VALENTINES AT THE FRONT

Valentine's Day anywhere the boys are,
Grouped around the sack that might as well be
Kicking like a caught thing, like a prisoner,
They sort it out so rapidly, then slowly.

They lean back amazed, then not at all amazed
At tissues ringed and arrowed to them. Plainly
This pattered here from home like a dim beast
Only the English feed. It would never guess

There is no place like home, and in home's place
Are these who sit befuddled in a fosse,
Crumpling the colour white and the colour pink
Away like news of some far Allied loss

That's one too many. Now they can only think
It's rained so long the past has burst its sides
And spilled into the future in the ink
Of untold villages of untold brides.

JUNE 31st, THE SOMME

My granddad held his nerve by mentioning me,
Lifting through his snapshots while his pals,
Like your granddad and yours, would focus slowly,
    Shells,

And dawn was like a dusk or at least all seven
Men had made of those two times an in-joke,
Making them both the same, so a day could never
    Quite break

On the First and another trick I believe yours had
Was to go 'June thirty-one!' It was getting blue though,
For all Great-Uncle Albert saying 'That?
    No,

It's dark, how many fingers am I holding?
You've no idea.' Then someone said 'It's a bit
Like in that book,' and the world shook with them nodding
    Albeit

The film was what they knew. The hour went misty,
Thin as the milk. Then day boiled up and the heat
Began. My granddad remembers feeling as ready
    Or not

As he was for my grandma once in a patterned room
They'd tidied. It was the one who would never know
Children who's said to have said when the sun came
    Out so

Unashamedly brightly, 'Nineteen-sixteen
Years since You gave a toss — well we're doing *this*,
As You can see!' They went off in a wobbly line,
    Forgot us.

[14]

LETTERS TO EDWARD THOMAS

for Derek Walcott

Dear Edward, just a note to say we're here
And nowhere could be better. And your key
Was where you said it would be, and the air
Is fresh with things you think, while looking kindly
On us intruders. Jenny says let's wait,
You can't be far away, while George of course
Has toppled into every single seat
To find his favourite. Five-to-one it's yours
He'll plump for, but Team Captain of the Cottage
Declares it's not allowed. I've said we're off
On a foraging expedition to the village
And that's where we are now, or soon enough
We shall be. We can't wait to see you, Edward.
We feel as if we have. I mean your home
Was breathing softly when we all invaded,
Not only air but breath, as in the poem
    I treasure that you showed me,
Which clings and flutters in me like a leaf
And falls when I remember how you told me
You couldn't write a poem to save your life!
    Consider that thing done.
Here's just a note to say we've been and gone.

❦

Dear Edward, just a note to say your wood
Has summoned us away, as you yourself
Hinted it might. The horde has swooped and fed
And drunk (in George's case three times) your health,
And Rose and Peter wouldn't hear of sleep,
Said it was banished back to Hampstead, swore
No path would go untrodden, and no sheep
Untroubled by us — George said: 'And no door
Of any inns unswung!' and so we're gone
A second time, though you'll have no idea
I wrote a first time. Blame the evening sun
For luring us back out. We love it here
And only you are missing. What that does
Is make us lonely. True, for all my chatter.
A beauty-spot will do that. What it has
Is one thing missing. Ask me what's the matter
        Anywhere it's beautiful
And there's your answer. Long before it's dark
You'll hear us creatures rolling up the hill
In twos, to be the last into your Ark,
        Or to be told by you
What things we missed, went by, lost, didn't do.

❦

Dear Edward, just a note to say today
The sun came in and scooped them up like eggs,
Our hearts, and set them fourteen miles away
And said now get there on your London legs —
So off we've gone, obedient, though sure
It's nothing but an agency of you,
And so I pin this to the master's door
In sure and certain hope you'll be there too,
With all our hearts at journey's end, in some
Vale of picnic-cloth. Last night we played
The word–games Adam taught to Eve, and some
Eve knew but never told him. Jenny made
A game of 'Where Was Edward?' which I won
By saying you were walking and had paused
To hear two nightingales — and not gone on
Until you'd taught them singing. This had caused
  The rumpus of all time
Amid the birds, which we could hear from here,
One saying 'Do we teach him how to rhyme?'
And all the rest as far as Gloucestershire
  Going 'Yes, don't you remember?'
George said you'd walked so fast it was November.

Dear Mr Thomas, now it's been so long
We lost your first name in the meadow grass
At dusk, when on a road we thought was wrong
We started recognising things. Your house
Then viewed us dimly. But you must excuse
The new meander in my messages,
And blame it on the elderflower juice
That George said would be *choice* with sandwiches
And seems so to have been. We all agree
We shall not leave tomorrow if our host
Insists on his invisibility,
And clears the table round us like a ghost
And seems to comment in the silences.
Rose and Peter have to leave, but George
Declares this week is cancelled, or his is.
Or so we can infer from how he snores.
      I tried to start some games
But after walking longer than we've ever
Who's in the mood for folding up the names
Of ones we know in town? Who cares whose lover
      Really cares for whom?
Our heads are bowed and spinning in the room.

❦

Dear Edward, just a note to say I left
A quiverful all weekend, in the hope
You'd sit down at your table. Here we laughed
And lolled for what seemed ages, and sat up
For what seemed scarcely time at all, but only
To see grey dawn arrive and blush to find us
Watching, late enchanted into early.
It's Monday noon and everything's behind us.
Rose and Peter took the six-fifteen,
As George and Jenny meant to. They at last
Boarded the nine o'clock, George in a dream
He started telling as the engine hissed,
Commissioning them for London. So I'm left
Abandoned to restore the place to how
It looked on that bright morning we arrived,
That seems so long ago. Time is so slow
        Without you. Then again
The moment that I shut the door, no doubt
You'll reach the gate and grin and ask me when
My friends are coming. I'll ask you about
        Your poems, as if you'd say,
Knocking the ashes from your favourite clay.

To punish you I threw the note away
I wrote you in your kitchen. Now my thanks
Are scribbled among strangers as we sway
Through Hampshire towards town, and the sun blinks
Behind the poplars. Edward Thomas, great
Unknowable, omniscient, your cottage
Waits for you: no sign we ever sat
Around your fire, no trace of pie or porridge,
Nor dreg of George's ale remains. No talks
Of ours will last the time you take to light
Your clay, and your first steps will make our walks
As brief and viewless as a shower at night.
These are our heartfelt thanks. We could have haunted
Many houses where we wouldn't see you.
At yours we thought it likely to be granted
Sight or sound, but it was not to be. You
     Were needed in the field,
By hawk or hedge, who knows, their need was greater
Than ours, who wanted names for things revealed
That we should know by now or may ask later.
     And reason not my need,
Who writes what nobody but she will read.

❦

Poem to Mr Thomas and Mr Frost,
Created by a dandelion you passed
As you in talk about a stanza crossed
Half Herefordshire, till you sat at last
In silence. I'm the dandelion that saw
Two aspens shake and shed in a quick wind,
And tried to loose her own leaves to the floor
Like they did and did manage in the end,
When they were both long gone in the great storm.
One to the west and one to the east, away
Towards the blood–commander in the dawn
And all his soldiers, pink becoming grey.
And you won't see this, if you live as long
As what you sent me: 'As the team's head-brass'
It starts but isn't titled. If I'm wrong
And your great hands one day are holding these
        Dandelion hairs,
The storm would not have come, the trees have kept
Their ground, and through the hearts of all the shires
Would Mr Thomas and Mr Frost have stepped
        And war like a rough sky
Been overlooked in talk, and blown on by.

🐛

Poem for Mr Edward Eastaway,
Who lives here care of me, so no one knows
His name is Rumplestiltskin and by day
He rips your verse to pieces in great prose.
By night he turns his prose to poetry
Because a poet told him to who saw
A mighty fine recruit for poverty
And wrote the line that opened his front door.
They have rejected Edward Eastaway
Again: the letter came this afternoon.
One knows precisely what a fool will say
Somehow. We've many stars to the one moon
In our night sky, but all that makes a face
Of that recurring rock is the one sun
It likes, without which it must find its place
To hide behind, or make believe it's gone.
         Edward Eastaway,
Whose name that isn't and whose time it ain't,
Who's living here or was just yesterday,
Or in Wales, Wiltshire, Oxfordshire or Kent,
         The rumour's that you crossed
The Channel. Stanza-break, sighs Mr Frost.

Dear Father Thomas, every Christmas Eve
Good children of the world are quite as shy
As I am to write *Dear* and then believe
For twenty lines our goodness could be why
It's worth our time. Our faith turns to this thread
That shuttles downward while the mischievous
Need nothing but a coalsack by the bed,
And wake to the same carols. Each of us
Is writing, Edward, asking the great space
Below us what is missing still, what gift
Will make us whole again. We fold and place
Our answers in the chimney and are left
These pink embarrassed authors by the fire.
We all talk tommy-rot we understand.
Somebody coughs, politely to enquire
Did they not kick a ball on No Man's Land
        Two years ago? 'That's so,'
Smiles Peter, adding: 'Not tonight, I fear.'
And I hear George's voice say: 'Cricket, though,
So Edward gets a knock.' But he's not here,
        George, he's where you are,
Restless tonight like all good children are.

One dead was sent a Valentine, so both
Were spared their lover's blushes. What I write
Is on its way nowhere, is less than breath,
So might be anything, as nothing might.
It's that there's nothing now that doesn't seem
As if it's where it ended. All the paths
Beyond this word or this become the same:
Thickets, or a handing-down of deaths
As by a school official, not a teacher,
A visiting official by one gate.
Now all the hope there is is in a picture
Of P. E. Thomas gone, because my fate
Is never to foresee, believed or no.
Is to be wrong. These words are packing up
And going. Words I mean you not to know
Don't see why they should move in any step
     I fix them with. So go,
You English words, while he's alive, and blow
Through all of him so Englishmen will know
You loved him and who cares how long ago,
     And hide him from the light
He'll strike and hold until his clay's alight.

❦

Dear Edward, when the war was over, you
Were standing where a wood had been, and though
Nothing was left for you to name or view
You waited till new trees had hidden you.
Then you came home and in a forest called
The Times your name was found, and not among
The officers but in a clearing filled
With verses, yours. Then your new name was sung
With all the old. And children leafing through
And old men staring and their daughters stilled
With admiration: all this happened too,
Or had already by the time you pulled
The book I hide this in from your top shelf
And blew its dust away. The year is what,
1930? '40? Please yourself,
But do remember as you smile and sit
    That everything's foreseen
By a good reader, as I think I am
On David's Day of 1917,
Reaching for blotting-paper. Now's the time
    To fold the work away
And find me on this bleak or brilliant day.

Choose me, Sie deutsche Worte. This is the first
Of all the letters you will never read,
Edward. I was shy in my own west
Always, so you never read a word
I sent, but this is written with as clear
A mind as has been opened like a shell.
'Greatly loved in the battery,' writes this dear
Major Lushington, who says you fell
In early morning with some battle won
And all the soldiers dancing. You were loved
In the battery and in the morning sun
Brought out the blessed clay, when something moved
Like cloud perhaps. The Major asked us round
To tell us you knew nothing. That your book
Of Shakespeare's Sonnets that they knelt and found
Was strangely creased and the clay didn't break
    Which Helen gave your son,
And Robert's *North of Boston* in your kit
They gave to me, not needing it. And when
They reached you you were not marked, not hit,
    Breeze blowing in your hair,
Chosen. What had stopped your heart was air.

Dear Edward, now there's no one at the end
There's nothing I can't say. Some eight or nine
I have by heart. Your farmer-poet friend
Is flying around the world on a fine line
That starts in you, or grows out from the days
You passed together. England is the same,
Cheering to order, set in its new ways
It thinks are immemorial. The Somme
Has trees beside it but some shovelwork
Will bring the dead to light. There's so much more
I want to say, because the quiet is dark,
And when the writing ends I reach a shore
Beyond which it's so cold and that's what changed,
Edward, on that Easter Monday. You
Were land to me, were England unestranged,
Were what I thought it had amounted to,
       But look at the fields now,
Look eyelessly at them, like the dug men
Still nodding out of Flanders. Tell them how
You walked and how you saw, and how your pen
       Did nothing more than that,
And, when it stopped, what you were gazing at.

Dear Edward Thomas, Frost died, I was born.
I am a father and you'd like the names
We gave our girl. I'm writing this at dawn
Where Robert lived, in Amherst, and your poems
I keep by his, his housebrick to your tile.
I teach you to my students, and aloud
I wonder what you would have come to. While
I wonder they look out at a white cloud
And so we pass the time. Perhaps I'll guess
Which one will ask me what they always ask:
Whom do I write for? Anybody? Yes,
You. And I'll walk home in the great dusk
Of Massachusetts that extends away
Far west and north, the ways you meant to go
To save your life. A good end to the day,
That's going to be. It's going to be cool, though,
    I see out in the town,
And start to turn the trees to what the world
Comes flocking here to see: eight shades of brown
Men never saw, and ninety-nine of gold,
    More shades than can have names,
Or names to bring them back when the snow comes.

HILLES, EDGE

A man has clambered up a hill so high
five counties hold their breath. There the air there is
is all his own and however far away
are farms and rivers they can all hear this.

He breathes again, his call unechoed. Winds
are pestering him with nothing. Soon enough
he takes a quarter-turn to look askance
and fixedly along the ridge, as if

to strike a balance between known and not,
between the dogged journey and the rest,
acknowledging the endlessness not yet,
scanning the close at hand for interest,

or at least a place to crouch in out of the wind
while the others scramble up. They will see in him
the mark of having seen. He will see in them
the awe he can now only understand.

THE ORDEAL

Acknowledged on our side of town,
        bragged of far from here, he'd been
our schoolfellow. He'd struggled in
        all but the soft options.

He'd struggled in the stuff that's meant
        to get us somewhere: History,
French. But from the windows
        we unbolted to hang out of

we would always see him racing
        round the dust of the chalk oval,
with one who Swiss-timed seriously,
        wanting the world warned.

I was among some eighteen
        to shoulder him home gleaming,
his sweat like a belonging, skin
        from somewhere new he came from,

and when he strolled out showered
        in a suit that was a watchword,
we made notes like the nobodies
        we grinned to see we were now,

now national talk was of him.
        No snapshot really caught it.
I am among the few who saw him
        up close and believe me.

He set himself what no one
        had imagined and we bet him,
which teamed us with the watches, made us
        sidekicks, I was kidding.

It teamed us with the ones who say
        Impossible! Too far!
The ones who say *The laws are laws,*
        alas! but hope they are.

It started when the gun cracked
        You're dead if he can do this.
Flashes went. We stood there,
        officialdom. When it was wholly

evident he couldn't do,
        the lid came off the subject,
and the night relaxed its grip
        for none ever thought it likely

and the fault was with him only.
        To have sought fault in the world,
to have tested it. We left then,
        ashamed to share his corner

though we took it in good humour
        at other towns we work in.
We set him further levels
        when we thought about him. Sometimes

you hear he smashed his record
        but he doesn't make the freeze-frame,
is not among the seven
        who relax across the line, or you will

hear he missed it narrowly
      in drizzle out at Iffley
if you happen to be passing
      through the business end of Oxford.

— Failing that a rustling
      in what passes for a forest
when the clock is on the warpath
      for a head-to-head in winter.

EDWARD WILSON

A dream of English watercolourists
all spread out on the hills: the sky is blue.
No breeze, nothing creative, not the least
exploratory dab. Then the same view

clouds and differs. Hills on the horizon
breed and open till the light has all
its colours boiling and there's only Wilson,
sketching in a blizzard, with his whole

blood sausage fist about a charcoal point,
grasping forever things in their last form
before the whiteness. A late English saint
has only eggs to save, himself to warm,

picturing Oriana. Lost winds
tug at the sketchbook. Shaded round, the eyes
Scott has to look at till tomorrow ends
are unenquiring and as blue as skies.

HURRY MY WAY

After the accident of rain all night,
The doctor's fingers tapping on the body:
That window first, then this and twice at that
For anything, but I until I'm ready
Am hiding in the folds of a wet Friday.
So I won't hurry your way. Hurry my way.

When work was handed out at morning break
In the watery warm school you also went to,
I drew the blank and blushed and had to make
The best of every silence I was sent to,
Trying to formulate a reason why they
Would always hurry their way. Hurry my way.

For 30,000 noons is how it strings
Together, this, it's really what you're roped to.
The rest is folding and unfolding things
You see, and free an arm to make a note to
See more of, but it's you against the tide. A
Wave is coming your way. Hurry my way.

And love was somewhere in the subterfuge
That suits it, but it had to come and get me.
The crowded room it glanced across was huge
And snow was falling by the time it met me.
It must have travelled each and every byway,
And that's what it calls hurry. Hurry my way.

Dark. I've not gone anywhere on this
Underworld of a day, but if you'd seen it
You wouldn't have done either. Happiness
Deters me from an ending, which may mean it
May have to make things harder soon. So I say
Whack on your winter coat and hurry my way.

OCTOBER SOUTH PLEASANT

The sugars congregated in this fuss of leaves
Don't show as many colours as the ways to die,

But about as many colours as the ways till now
We've written how that happens. What this one believes

Is out there there's a tree of colour only I
Imagine different. When I point it out, don't stare,

Remark or disagree or don't in fact be there;
I'll lower my arm in time and make a note somehow.

CALAIS

They tin-opened his head.
Apparently it said
CALAIS across his brain
in red. Which should explain
the puzzlement and pain
and focus that he felt,
that afternoon he smelt
its fuel-and-fishy air,
then mulled it over in a square

like one whom little girls
untasselling their hair
in French and combing it to curls
adore when he's thirteen,

who wonders what on earth they mean
and guesses and is wrong,
goes pink and carries on,
finds the ferry gone.

MOONCALVES

A local beauty known to the police,
She was invited in but allowed home
Unmolested. A credit to their force,
They were. She declined a ride and made her own

Meticulous way back across the sea.
The officers were glad to note at first
How ruffled she appeared, her dignity
Patched and cobbled somehow, or at least

They started glad then stiffened as she strolled,
Growing impressive out there, and the young
Detective said he knew her and the old
Desk-sergeant said *We none of us do, son,*

And out on the horizon their poor eyes
Were taken, where a million kinds of girl
Bewildered them to blinking, but the lies
They told each other were identical.

Mooncalves. It wouldn't take a crime
To bring her in, they joked in a corridor,
Pasting up her picture. Ask what time
It was they'd slap and bellow *Time for more!*

Home they went that morning with her face
Still bothering them between the houses. She
Was known to them, they were prepared to stress,
Were anybody wondering was she.

CREAK

I needed to write a note to her. I'd needed
Train times and clothes and magazines for weeks now
But today to write a note to her and it's true
I scarcely knew her. Overnight, it looks like,
I must have become orbited, and sprouted
Oceans that would whisper as she passed me,
Or waver, glad and sideways, none the wiser,
Then furrow, dimly knowing in the daytime.
I needed to write a note to her, to begin
A scale I could master quickly and descend on
Once risen on and learn its minor too,
For bone Sunday.
                        I wrote a note to her
That splattered into rhyme against my wishes.
So I scrunched it up and said if it hits the bin
There's going to be a relationship. It missed it,
And meaning nothing circled to a halt,
An avoided iceberg, the origami for *rubbish*.
I was settling down to a skim through magazines
When it started to creak apart like an old fist
Too weak to clench for long, and by the time
The creaking stopped a note was there again,
A pale green leaf as smooth as now my brow was,
A second draft, an effort which not only
Got written, it got folded, licked and posted,
And triggered what had had to be discharged
While there was time to hold it, have and miss it.

But the first note has been stooped for and unravelled,
And ever since hides in a drawer in wrinkles,

Brown and furred and saying it told me so
Like a dear retainer whose love I could never dodge
And wouldn't now. Which explains why I would never
Tell him we both ended up with others
In time, and without his or any English.

THE STUNNING

We must pause and throw our collective arms around
The really stunning. Because it is not their time now

And the look they give us is guilty but unsure of
Precisely the offence. As they recall it

They formerly met in sets by lawn or water,
Could see through clouds to the next one and arrive there,

Knew much about themselves, what they had sprung from,
What was expected and when, had super timing,

Skilled repartee, knew a good thing when they sipped it,
Recalled what hadn't hurt, and felt they were truly

Tucked and treasured. Don't ask us what undid that
And shook them up so badly, but it's different:

We're lucky if we see them. A few strict faces
In magazines, they aren't them. Those who do that

Look ordinary at a lunch, look bothered, active,
They brush the sun off their freckled shoulders and aren't them.

Of whom we mean we get mere flashes and glimpses.
They may close a book in a bay window in summer,

Explaining it barely in earshot, or suddenly go,
Cinch their bags and be off, the moment we make

The overdue book desk. They will rush the leaves
Like anyone in the autumn but their companions

Do all the talking. One place we can spot them
Is any doorway we watch any duo do

The get-in-the-way-to-the-right-and-the-left-now tango,
Till they know each other as well as two ever want to,

Must slink on by in shame. Often we've seen them
Cramped in the backs of cars then waving forth

New compilation tapes to concerned lovers.
And we heard them getting obvious directions

We could have given them had we got there sooner.
We last saw the really stunning high in the stadium,

Shrilly supporting a side from nowhere near them,
Twining a sky-blue scarf like a shy bell-ringer,

Gazing in awe at the keeper long after he cleared it.
Bad language made them turn, they clapped if we did.

That the match was lost in the end seemed to mean nothing.
We passed this close: they looked engrossed in the programme.

These days we have no idea how the really stunning
Are sleeping, or how they make do, or how they will ever

Regroup and be reconciled, or if they will even
Listen when we ourselves have plucked up courage

To tell them they are forgiven, there's really nothing
To forgive. They may take some convincing.

HIDE AND SEEK

Of all the things to win at. There I am,
Immobilised except for my young gut,
Which does its jellyfish and does its clam
Because you've come to double-check the hut:

And the relief is evangelical
That I can breathe again and show my face,
Until all other faces show that all
Are found and mine was the last hiding-place;

Then many draw to it as to a shrine,
In glum approval, jealous but sincere,
That of the silences you favoured mine,
And the last thing that mattered mattered here.

HIS FIRST MINUTE

After noon is Night, we'd done in English,
And differed on its merits in her room,
One saying what the other said was rubbish
And looking up or going to do that soon,

Before too long a gap could breed the germ
It had just done. I went on with our language,
Leaning against her on a train that term
One Saturday, and pointing out that cottage

Thatched and white, some way from all the other
Homes and village shops, or an inn we might
Frequent if this was where we were. I asked her
What she thought of it, as she fell her height

In bliss. She glanced back from her look away
And reasoned as she read that it was fine
As country goes but small and anyway
Too near the railway. 'Yes, but if this line,'

I ventured, 'wasn't here' — I saw the oxbow
Lake of our illogic trickle dry —
'Then how could we have seen the place, you know,
Not being here,' she asked, and caught my eye.

THE HEAT CAME OUT

The heat came out and spread a cloth as wide
As it would float on our fresh shattered grass.
It ploughed our foreheads, beaded us in cars,
Grilled avenues, made galleries of shade,

And was not moving anywhere we said
Was good, and could be got to in a day, say,
Or kind (we tried to fib the heat away)
Or somewhere it belonged. Instead it stayed,

Untangling us, exhibiting us younger,
Resetting us by streams or banked up high
In tens of all-agreeing thousands. Why
It did this we would have to ponder later,

Indoors from sudden rain. Was it too clear
This time, our prayer for it to come, the heat?
And so it came on all four blistered feet
And dying for our praise? When it got here

We hated it already. Nothing there is
Prepares us for what comes, and, as the thunder
Smells and destroys itself, we sip and wonder
If anything prepares what comes for us.

DEEP SORRINESS ATONEMENT SONG

for missed appointment, BBC North, Manchester

The man who sold Manhattan for a halfway decent bangle,
He had talks with Adolf Hitler and could see it from his angle,
And he could have signed the Quarrymen but didn't think they'd
make it
So he bought a cake on Pudding Lane and thought 'Oh well I'll
bake it'

> But his chances they were slim,
> And his brothers they were Grimm,
> And he's sorry, very sorry,
> But I'm sorrier than him.

And the drunken plastic surgeon who said 'I know, let's enlarge 'em!'
And the bloke who told the Light Brigade 'Oh what the hell, let's
charge 'em,'
The magician with an early evening gig on the *Titanic*,
And the Mayor who told the people of Atlantis not to panic,

> And the Dong about his nose,
> And the Pobble *re* his toes,
> They're all sorry, really sorry,
> But I'm sorrier than those.

And don't forget the Bible, with the Sodomites and Judas,
And Onan who discovered something nothing was as rude as,
And anyone who reckoned it was City's year for Wembley,
And the kid who called Napoleon a shortarse in assembly,

> And the man who always smiles
> 'Cause he knows I have his files,
> They're all sorry, truly sorry,
> But I'm sorrier by miles.

[46]

And Robert Falcon Scott who lost the race to a Norwegian,
And anyone who's ever spilt the pint of a Glaswegian,
Or told a Finn a joke or spent an hour with a Swiss-German,
Or got a mermaid in the sack and found it was a merman,
       Or him who smelt a rat,
       And got curious as a cat,
       They're all sorry, deeply sorry,
       But I'm sorrier than that.

All the people who were rubbish when we needed them to do it,
Whose wires crossed, whose spirit failed, who ballsed it up or blew it,
All notchers of *nul points* and all who have a problem Houston,
At least they weren't in Kensington when they should have been at
                                    Euston.

       For I didn't build the Wall
       And I didn't cause the Fall
       But I'm sorry, Lord I'm sorry,
       I'm the sorriest of all.

HOME FROM A CLOSE READING

Excuse how late we are, or how our once white sleeves
Are twisted into tourniquets that turn our forearms
Bulbous and excuse our pulling off our gloves
    And boots and dragging out
    Our stools towards the flames.
We are home from a close reading of each other's names.

There's much left smoking of it, of the National Hall.
It tips its roof and cackles in the dented square,
The roguish uncle even children know is well
    Exposed. Whole cabinets
    Stood balanced on a stair,
Till the dead washed from their lockers and got everywhere.

We bustled to our corners in the alphabet. That's why
My enemies have surnames much like mine. I spent
On marble floors on hands and knees the longest day
    In history with them. I'd
    Believed them innocent,
However fat their files seemed, what in fact that meant.

Don't get me wrong, like my file gets me very wrong,
At least on its concluding page. Don't go away
Assuming I've done half the things it says: I've done
    The lot. I could have told
    The next tribunal that,
But now who'll care? Its authors won't against a wall

That's crackled at. Now all the doubt there ever was
Out-hints the constellations. From the countryside
Come more in carts to learn what Freedom is. Because
    It's in those ruins or is if
    You scrabble hard and good.
You find out what it did about you when it could.

AND INDIANS

They made a word for light when it went out,
Then many words for dark, if not such dark
As fell and spread among them like a doubt.

It's not a date we celebrate, but then
There's no one day to ring or week to mark.
It happened and keeps happening to them.

Nothing to make a song or dance about.
Nothing to be the theme of a third act.
They had no argument and show no sign

Of coming back to make one. They were *them*,
And death is in that word like its own wine
Gone acid and eroding them to *then*.

Then to the fled allotment of a time.
Then to the listed ruin of a fact.

BACK GARDENS IN EARLY MORNING

It's cold in the tall gardens of the well-to-do
as the lights come on, at first two crimson spots
of guarded dens, below them the bland squares
of bedrooms one by one come up like numbers,
so bright together they can set the dawn back.
Soon kitchens fuss and flicker on like court cards,
hearts and diamonds, crossed by a boy or a woman
who looking out would see you at this window
if she ever looked out. Small in upper corners
the misted pinks of bathrooms, each with a monster's
pixellated silhouette for a while,
then not, so suddenly you start to feel
it could have walked the wet grey wilderness
of the lawn below, got in your flat behind you.
You even chance a cautious tête-à-tête
with your haggard old reflection — he's been up
all night — to scan the lawn for ghosts. Your twin
peers in your room. He too comes up with nothing.
You both sit back and fade and let the hoop
of nothing skelter round you to your slippers.
Other people's gardens, and all gardens
in winter and our gardens when we leave home
go with us like the rest of every brain,
the rest you must and have no time to learn,
the rest that rustles when you barely notice.
Fetching a ball from flowers you'd have heard it
a first time, or unearthing at the edges
of bonfires someone's toy that can't be yours,
some kneeling melted rifleman with the face
of Punch: that calls from somewhere farther out

than you can bear and must go on the fire
with all the rest. A sense you never were
is lodged in gardens with the sense you're gone
like gardens either side. Now is a time
you sense it and high windows are a place.
You may well find it's gone when you get closer,
like anything, and leaves you in your state
of knowingness, that fortified small state
we'll visit once of course, like one of Wales's
crumbled castles. Other people's gardens
close with a viral urgency on places
anyone knows everything. You see men
cease to learn, you hear them swear an oath,
forbid a word, accept an honour, rise
to end all argument. Then rest assured
a garden far away is made aware,
and prospers at its edge in that direction.
The stillest garden is the fastest moving.
Its sweat is stonework and the wage is flowers.
It sets its records by a grassy ruin,
where a guidebook is a sure sign the hedges
are circling you, and a smile from the cake lady
is the one you give the old, or in your moments
of local grace may beam at a grave in sunshine.
I look down into other people's gardens.
Across, old as the trees but long in thrall
to things that go against us, hangs the black
top-hatted lamp of one who could afford it,
shining where there's no one now it's winter,
its cloud of visitations long departed
to August, that far trouble-spot of empire.
Bits of the dead are dotted on the glass
like mystifying crotchets of what thing
sang to them and drew them and for now

exhibits them well-lit by the cold house.
More lights go on and lower in those homes
then off again and the sky is screen white,
doodled on by nudging branches high
as aerials and the day has long begun.
You would have to wait a thousand times as long
as I intend to for that lamp to blink.
Square that again to see a back door open
and people make their way into these gardens.

THE ROOM

The room was his and said so, and its reds
and greens and yellows were as close as brothers.
He bashed about the place, and he trailed stories
　　　and he had two matching beds
　　　　　to choose from.

The room was his and furiously quiet
at times or he would loosen to a demon
in company, be lit from down below,
　　　let others grope for light
　　　　　to see by.

The room was his and empty, so his mother
tamed the walls to various subtle pastels
very close in shade but cold and ruffled
　　　to have to have each other
　　　　　to sit with.

The room was spare and either bed or both
were needed and the top of the draped table
had spectacles, an earring and old water.
　　　He found a floating moth
　　　　　to mention.

The room was small and bedless, with a desk
the drawers of which slid out to present nothing.
Eight paperbacks of various kinds were always
　　　there that he might ask
　　　　　to borrow.

The room was quite immaculate, the help
from Melbourne, her credentials fine, her manner
rude and steady and she read bestsellers
     and forced the window up
          to smoke from.

MR F GETS FIT

Homage to the Presiding Spirit of Amherst

I jogged away from town on a dim day
That didn't know me, though I knew my way,
Or thought as much. The way seemed unimpressed
And thought it ought to put me to some test,

For not one path I confidently chose
But steepened. If I slackened then they rose,
And took my breath as if they needed air
For mischief and had singled out my share.

Like I was someone that today could spare.
Make light of, brush away, not its affair.
One that today could do its work without,
Be fond of, being unconcerned about.

On these new ways by which I had to pass
Came none with any notion who I was,
But all, by light too brief for friendship found,
Suggested I begin by turning round,

So I should face where I belonged: elsewhere.
But I had run too much from here to there
Not to prefer to walk from there to here,
As I began to do, not to appear

Unneighborly to neighbors. And it took
Ten times as long, by any watchman's book,
And no less upward than it was before.
As if the toll is always to be more

To gain admittance at a snow-white gate,
And tread the stony path in no fit state
For any sight but mine. So I doubt if I
Shall jog again this side of a white sky.

But I may get intolerably heated
Should you so much as mutter that I cheated.
I woulda jogged forever if I coulda.
It did me good. I hope it does you gooder.

THE ELBOW PEOPLE

Let's hand it to the Elbow People. Theirs
Is to stand unexcited on the stairs
Glancing across the camera at what?
A camera that's not there or is but not
Taking them: The Elbow Camera.
You don't smile for the Elbow Camera.

You can't take anything away from Hatgirl.
It's all been taken by the usual uncle.
Get too close, her body starts to slim
Until it's what it was when she knew him.
Her eyes are sandy with her teddy-bears
When Elbow Husband nudges her upstairs.

You might recall the Honourable Member
For where we were, one of a growing number
Dead each time we're back from a long lunch
Then spotted rising from an empty bench
Delighted! Elbow People will remind him
Gently if they find him and they find him.

Rats and That come every night in coaches
Eating as they sing and sporting watches
Promised them. They're only miles away
When without fail the Elbow Motorway
Slings them home digesting to the sewers
To work as Elbow Listeners, Elbow Viewers.

Yet it's no secret all of us derive
From Ankle Ancestors who when alive
Looked different from the way you'd care to now.
But then in photos all the same somehow.
Like this one, this stiff grouping at a Ball:
Idiots, elbows of no use at all.

Now Elbow People clip into their cars,
Explaining you can't judge that time by ours,
Though as the window sinks they lean and say
Or vice versa. Then they crunch away
Conferring as the window glints and climbs.
We were a picture, slanted in the frames.

Hand it to the Elbow People then.
Surprisingly approachable young men,
Lifting drinks and listening with a smile
Then tapping your ideas into a file
That had, you notice, got them anyway.
Down the hatch. Today is Elbow Day.

CARNIVAL BAHIA

We're here in a shade of white for a time of prayer
but you wouldn't think that, not with the fire and the works of the
fireworks,
and not with the ones we're with whose state of unthinking is to be
dancing,
from which not the little hints of the gods and girls can always shake
them —

We're here in a net of stars as a catch of peace
but you'd never know that, not with the heart and the beat of the
heartbeat —
this is the start of the struggle that starts when the catch is netted
and teeming
and seeing the life in all things that are seeing the life at last in
things —

We're here in a street of eyes to a house of hands
but you'd never see that, not with the eye and the lash of the eyelash,
and none can move in the crowd, which is bound to mean the crowd
is moving
somewhere that matters now and will always matter somewhere to
many —

We're here on a page of light in a book of none
but you won't have read that, not by the moon and the light of the
moonlight —
by dawn you will, when the wind and white and black of the passing
daytimes
are only the riffling back for the lost place of the only reader.

THE FIRE-ANTS

Look who was standing in a loaf of ants
Eight seconds, whose attempt at a kick-dance
Was excellent, whose trainer was alive
On close inspection and whose sock a hive,
Who gripped the air! — The guide got there and thumped
My trailing foot until the blighters jumped
And fell. Fire-ants, they were, like scraps of earth,
Conferring as they dropped, reporting *Death*
To the workers who not looking went *It's not*
To which was added *If it is so what*
By the intelligentsia of the nest.
Their task it is to quibble and know best.

Mine was to bop one-legged for a while
Until the guide stood up with the right smile.
Good to have got out quickly, was his gist.
I didn't disagree. That was some dust
Had come alive. The guide was moving off,
So I trod some half a dozen into scuff
Then lightly squatted down to watch them cope
With coming to this pass. I saw one grope
And topple out intact and crab around
In chaos till it found its proper ground,
Then lope away, infernally askew.
A dance it isn't, what we have to do.

THE FLOTILLA

New Year's Day, Baia de Todos os Santos, Salvador, Bahia

The fireworks freckle again in the bright sunlight
        over the great flotilla of which our white boat
    is proudly part, and we've on board no less
than Salvador's premier firework-maker, he looks

why he looks like Picasso and tilts that terrapin head
        in fair concern at the pepper and bang of these arts
    of newcomers — to illuminate of all things
the morning after, the dolts! he sighs; I wonder

what would they say of our boat amid so many
        out on the Bay of All Sins at the top of the year?
    being on it how can we say? we devote the moments
to seeing who else is out (who isn't this morning?) —

For a start, there's the thin black boat of the Sacred something
        downing and upping along with a picnic awning
    sheltering eight big clerics in flapping outfits
while sixteen seventeen jostling G and S sailors

are doing the crewing, they're there,
        and most of the crews, from the boats inclining to being
    ships to the boats conceding they're largely dinghies,
are keeping the one explicably bloodshot eye

on the boat of the Sacred something (the guide did say)
        because it's going where the whole flotilla is going;
    it's the verb to its meaning,
it's the modest genius to its movement,

it calls the shots which come in sevens and suchlike
        for prim historical reasons from brown cannons,
    but the whole sea is sprinkled with good boats now,
boats to tell you about,

boats of the great flotilla this bright morning.
        There's the boat of course of the lookalikes:
    the Pope, another Picasso, Gandhi and Groucho,
except, as we near that boat, the opposite happens

this New Year's Day and they seem to get closer and closer
        to whom they seem, the closer you get, until
    it's got to be them and the only way it can't be
is that it can't be, it can't be! we're more than a little

relieved when right in between progresses the sloop
        of eleven straw-hatted husbands, fanned and sleeping,
    dreaming a twelfth who's happy to munch and steer it,
a common belief, but they can't go far wrong really

in the great flotilla. There's the stripy boat of those
        who reckon the snickering flags on the boats are nations
    not letters of the alphabet, what they do is
call amicably in foreign tongues all morning

from small fat books they purchased for this purpose,
        Portuguese-Anything Anything-Portuguese
    glossaries, they clop them shut and deliver
perfect salutations to the sea-wind,

then wave their own flag people think means *fever*.
        There is by chance one foreign vessel among us
    now gathered up in the fleet, it's the raft of loners:
they think Brazil has unilaterally opted

to steal away, one grows a cautious thumb. I like
            the boat of men in tops they got for Christmas,
        amazingly all the same mauve shiny top,
so people guess they're vacationing officials

and sail on wisely parallel with a smile;
            now tinkling by is the quiet boat of those
        who have with no little skill concealed the fact
they don't like soccer, can't dance, turn in early —

they're only *pretending* to yawn, they'll set us all off;
            there's a brilliant pun in the name of this grey-green craft
        that's gliding by and it takes three minutes to get it,
but we do, so laughter starting and dying is all

that crew can hear, they perhaps feel liked if always
            out of reach; alongside I believe
        we have the boat of the busily filling in their
diaries: in that oblong with the words

NEW YEAR'S DAY they are writing 'New Year's Day,
            went out on a great Flotilla', they suck big pens,
        look up, confirm this thing they have got in writing;
there's a boat of dignitaries, it's been violently polished:

they wave at the people on other boats, who wave
            back: the dignitaries do not see they are in
        a time of waving, they think it's them; there's a boat
of these who swim and samba: each of the beauties

believes he is or she is unique in height,
            like Jesus only not that height, and here comes
        the boat of those who are victims of a prank
considered since Halloween by the little sister

[64]

of one of them, they thought they were in a room
            sipping *cachaca*, now she has settled the whole fleet
        hilariously upon them like a necklace,
and she's ashore in the city, asleep, avenged. Watch

for the boat that's steadying nearest the beach, that boat
            thinks it's about to be leader, thinks it's the swallow
        to go with when the flight wheels, but then so does
the boat that's farthest out in the Bay, the speedboat, see

it's poised, soon to be leader. They are both wrong:
            the movement is always across, they will always be
        flanking the way things go, they always
stay far from the central Sacred boat of whatever

the guide said earlier. That about does it for boats:
            the others are all the boats without any obvious
        linking aspect, I therefore pass over those boats,
except to say they are lovely to be among,

and each could tell if you asked its mate or mascot
            what our proud white boat really looks like, and what thing
        brings us together on this with our firework-maker,
whether it's what we say or the thing about us

that can't be helped, it could be some comic element —
            then we could be safe and easy to find in our own boat,
        if one who knew nothing was here and was asking for us,
stepping among the barques of the great flotilla,

for there's no clear factor in common or bet we're the best for,
            though enough do seem to have chosen us for their time
        in the Bay of All Sins this morning: I'll be surprised
if no one turns from the rail in a while to explain that.

RIO NEGRO

As a boy awake in bed with a mum's kiss
He wipes can clearly see the wedge of light
He needs will thin away from him, the darkness
Falls on the uncomprehending. Night

Swallows this observation, and this male,
Curled and sailing farther than it felt
Possible away from what felt whole,
Is stretching for a handhold on the world.

The Rio Negro, nothing for a view,
Its banks in blackness like whatever things
Nor and Neither are referring to,
Bats my breath away with its slow wings.

Too weak to say I miss you, I've about
The scope of what I started with, the sliver
Of matter immaterial without
What plumps for it in just so dark a river.

I'm glad you saw me. Now you'd see me shift
Gingerly to stern to watch a sky
Stubbed by that hot city that we left
Ten hours ago. I'm glad you caught my eye.

Macaws I saw stay in the mind. They soared
And tilted in the least of the old light
Over the treetops. If you see this bird
Among us it's been scissored from the mate

It would have flown beside for sixty years.
My cabin-window's black as the reply
Of rivers to the I and its ideas,
Eroding them to barely one, but I

[66]

At least am moving, like the Rio Negro,
Somewhere coming helplessly to light,
And even nothing, signing itself zero,
Is paying homage like a satellite.

LULLABY OF THE THAMES

Now you are in my life, my insomniac,
I'll spare you some of this from the deep gardens.
Yours, your sleep I'd make like how the black
Unsmiling river turns and stretches, widens
Or narrows, knowing nothing of its names,
Or how it rose and why, or that all around
New days burst open, hurting. Like the Thames
Your sleep I'd have long, easy, grey, east-running,
With a light dirt of dream where it meets ground.

FOR MY DAUGHTER

If I call this poem that, I have as new
A pattern of three words to learn as you
Have everything. The day you get the gist
Of what this is becoming you'll have missed
The point you were. Then you'll have reached the stage
You stay at, insofar as every age
In writing is a step along a shelf
Where words are stowed and weather like a self.
The height is dizzy but it stays the same
And the ladder gets there when you make a name
Of something I keep calling you. That date
We won't forget, are bound to celebrate,
Like rain we needed after a long spell
Of what was blissful but incredible.

THE RHYMES

Back in the indescribable condition

birds fluttered down and pecked. She had already
learned how stillness kept them. She knew also
nearness rushed them off, you could wave arms
and flap them very far from here, how far now!

Back in the indescribable condition

birds fluttered down and stayed and nothing moved them.
No time or fright, no motion or surprise. They went
everywhere it all went. Her first word
was one of them. Then they hid away like wings.

UNDER THESE LIGHTS

i.m. Joseph Brodsky

You who had dared me out under these lights
Have left them alone I see now my eyes accustom.

Gone, though your voice is hung in the heights of the ballroom,
A flex of vowels slung on a crown of hooks.

You don't have to love us now, and the leaves of books
Are flicking aloud on the lens of the first reader

To hear you from the future. I remember
That was the sound I heard, though you who made it

Were working a joke in then, like you'd decided
We knew you were only passing, weren't local,

Were out to upset us somehow. That was that chuckle:
Something to do with oxygen, fair pain,

Oasis reached at last, though knowing each sign
One could survive was not a sign for home.

ON A DEVON ROAD

Whatever thoughts there were for me on a Devon road,
nothing knotted them suddenly to one spot
like what lay up ahead, flopped and brownish,
too much of it for a bird, too much for a fox;
one wound as I went by its snouted head
had trickled; the slightest movement was beyond it.

It was a badger. I looked back over my shoulder
twice at it and a third time turned, I was staring:
its stillness had a force and a beat that nothing
green remotely had. It was pulsing
with having been. It was not what was around it:
where it and the world met was a real edge —

like someone thumping 'badger' to the page
with a finger and old Remington had banged
a hole with b clean through, and couldn't mend it,
that dumb dot in his title word, and had to
use his hand to stop light coming through it.

PORTOBELLO

When you were the one reading
My palm, in the second hour of our one life,

And I, sitting back for good and noticing white stuff
Suddenly falling on Portobello and staying,

You couldn't for all the books in the world have learned
More than one watching us,

Who buttered his torn roll, and in any case
I cared what the lines were meaning on my hand

(Of what's to come, and when, and why that)
About as much as I cared what they meant on yours:

What mattered was who was reading it,
And whose it was;

I mean, when I look at the stars it isn't the stars
I'm looking at.

ALFIE'S LULLABY

On a day
    When I lay
Where I used to forever

And the voices
    I was watering
Were in flower as I rose

Then I
    In the fields
With the clouds in my fingers

Could sing
    Till the sun
Was a road on the sea

CAP D'AIL

The chap on the next promontory began
and finishing presented to your mother
an oil of her bright villa in the sunshine
that she enjoyed enough to frame and mount there

and here it is still, after everything,
save our own honeymoon and the sea's latest
rash assault on rocks. One bay along
the artist lived, some Englishman. The coast

was dotted with them once, vague amateurs
all kicking out their easels to the east
and starting up, a chain of volunteers
defending something, aged and unmissed.

Too woken up, too hot I came down here
to watch the sunlight widen to sunshine
and grow oppressive, like a fine idea
becomes unquestioned and begins to burn,

and spread so fast and far it is the cause
of any act. It blazes like an *A*,
elates its fans and levers off the doors
of all the neutrals. Then it has its day.

It will within an hour render this whole
area beyond me. While I can
I face it, a petitioner for the pale,
my people's crosses freckling my skin.

You fled here as a child, down to this spot,
not France, the south, the town, the property
but here, out on the Point, with only rock
between you and the freedom of the sea.

[75]

This early free it is, though money blooms
abroad in ever bigger yachts all day,
and villas heap behind me, piled like tombs
together, ostentatious, empty.

This little L-shaped bench where you looked out
was refuge for you when the time was wrong.
Rich with plans and dreamy but without
defence, you waited to be noticed gone.

That child in your old portrait is a sigh
in ribbons, with the features of a doll,
while in her eyes Versailles upon Versailles
sweep over the horizon like a scroll,

and here you sat. A wave assails the rock
and never learns. All day the merguez-brown
boys will climb and dare each other off,
grin, turn pensive, suddenly be gone

and hit the water hidden. Nothing yet.
No one. Not the unlatching of a window
yet. It's fresh and quiet as the sheet
before the brush is knelt in the deep yellow.

I climb the classic steps into the house,
out of a place where air is fire for me
to tread the ocean that the inside is,
unbreathing unfamiliarity.

This place has heard some things, and by your look
last night you heard them. All I feel is dew
of what transpired, a last fling from a dark
I wipe away and do this thing for you.

Exempt from local memory I pass
untapped between the walls. The atmosphere
parts to let me by like a Red Cross
bearer floating through a barrage. War

has pity for the ones affecting nothing:
memory less so. I amble round
and round the skull of this old villa. Nothing
speaks. My name escapes without a sound,

I stop. The silk screens in the living room
are Japanese scenes: scarlet, green and black.
Gold's to them as white is to this poem,
the light that was and waits and will come back

at the last tassel's end. The screens have stains,
dim but indelible, at pains to say
what happened on some long-lost afternoons
among you. You remember anyway.

Her books are as they were, the first editions
regiments. No order to relax
will come. Along the shelf the Harold Robbins
fade and fatten till they wreck their backs.

The painting of the villa's in the hall.
Violet for the rocks, the sea the blue
of birds' eggs, dirty somehow, and the whole
as I close in the way I shouldn't do

is crust and flake, moon-acreage of oil
I'm not supposed to see. I rest my cheek
right by it like a brute, and then recoil
to the right distance and the way we look.

I hear the waves come in while seeing his
rough smear of them, and from one shuttered dot
you waking up. A week of memories
we have ourselves now. Nothing, but a start.

Some stormy clouds are dabbed above the villa,
as if it spawned them. I can see the artist
pink and pondering as he stirs a colour,
trying to do your mother something honest,

dear, though if she pictured you today
the sky would be as blue as it is now,
with every window open to the bay
and you at one so she could see you how

I do. I shiver and my name is called.
My pages lift, I flatten them. The breeze
slams a door and silence asks whose fault
that was and silence answers nobody's.

DAWN ON THE MIDI

In the one pink hour these villas
have to themselves before the English voices;
in the time before the couple
start winding back the eyelids of the windows,
I pass as close as one who needs to see them
can pass to the lost owners

who are riding the end carriage
of the Blue Train to the sheet of light they'd fashioned
to flutter for a time
between them and a future that was waiting
politely by, with hands as disinclined
to mercy as a clock's are,

or smiling at the window
of the First Class then running backwards waving
saddened into smoke though —
two sights she wakes from on a lip of light
and ribbon and remembers where she is now,
mid-afternoon in heaven,

and soon to be seen stepping
the marble staircase, all the hood and fuss
with the viewfinder crucial,
while the twelve at lunch or whist beside the palm-tree
go quiet as now, passing as close as any
who won't see you can pass

to you who note them plainly,
or me in this bird-yellow hour these houses
have to themselves, while the breeze
has breath enough to puff the toys in races
across our idle and impulsive pool,
stone-deaf to the sea breaking.